NO LONGER PROPERTY OF
ANYTHINK LIBRARIES/
RANGEVIEW LIBRARY DISTRICT

D0132517

Pebble® Plus

DINOSAURS
VELOCIRAPTOR

A 4D Book

by Tammy Gagne

PEBBLE
a capstone imprint

Download the Capstone 4D app!

- Ask an adult to download the Capstone 4D app.

- Scan the cover and stars inside the book for additional content.

When you scan a spread, you'll find fun extra stuff to go with this book! You can also find these things on the web at www.capstone4D.com using the password: veli.95476

Pebble Plus is published by Pebble,
1710 Roe Crest Drive, North Mankato, Minnesota 56003
www.mycapstone.com

Copyright © 2019 by Pebble, a Capstone imprint. All rights reserved. No part of this publication may be reproduced in whole or in part, or stored in a retrieval system, or transmitted in any form or by any means, electronic, mechanical, photocopying, recording, or otherwise, without written permission of the publisher.

Library of Congress Cataloging-in-Publication Data
Names: Gagne, Tammy, author.
Title: Velociraptor : a 4D book / by Tammy Gagne.
Description: North Mankato, Minnesota : an imprint of Pebble, [2019] |
Series: Pebble plus. Dinosaurs | Audience: Age 4–8.
Identifiers: LCCN 2018003061 (print) | LCCN 2018009267 (ebook) |
ISBN 9781515795599 (eBook PDF) | ISBN 9781515795476 (hardcover) |
ISBN 9781515795537 (paperback)
Subjects: LCSH: Velociraptor—Juvenile literature.
Classification: LCC QE862.S3 (ebook) | LCC QE862.S3 G3383 2019 (print) |
DDC 567.912—dc23
LC record available at https://lccn.loc.gov/2018003061

Editorial Credits
Hank Musolf, editor; Charmaine Whitman, designer;
Kelly Garvin, media researcher; Laura Manthe, production specialist;
Illustrator, Capstone Press/Jon Hughes

Design Elements
Shutterstock/Krasovski Dmitri

Note to Parents and Teachers

The Dinosaurs set supports the national science standards related to life science. This book describes and illustrates velociraptor. The images support early readers in understanding the text. The repetition of words and phrases helps early readers learn new words. This book also introduces early readers to subject-specific vocabulary words, which are defined in the Glossary section. Early readers may need assistance to read some words and to use the Table of Contents, Glossary, Read More, Internet Sites, Critical Thinking Questions, and Index sections of the book.

Printed and bound in China.
000309

Table of Contents

Meet the Velociraptor

Velociraptor was small but fast. Adults could run 40 miles (64 kilometers) per hour in short bursts. That is about the speed cars drive in the city.

Velociraptor stood 3 feet (0.9 meter) tall. It weighed up to 33 pounds (15 kilograms). It was about the size of a turkey.

This dinosaur was birdlike. It had feathers on its short front legs. But velociraptor could not fly.

The Speedy Thief

The name *velociraptor* means "speedy thief." Velociraptor was a carnivore. It had three claws on each front foot.

It had a large claw on each back foot. It used them for hunting meat. The claws helped it catch prey quickly.

Velociraptor Fossils

Velociraptor lived about 70 million years ago. Velociraptor fossils have been found in Asia. Most were buried deep in the desert.

Dinosaur fossils have been found with velociraptor bite marks. The marks match its widely spaced teeth.

On the Hunt

Scientists think this species hunted in packs. Velociraptor fossils have been found together with prey. They could have been fighting over the food.

Velociraptor was also a scavenger. The dinosaur ate meat left by other animals. It ate eggs.

Glossary

fossil—bones or other remains of a long dead animal or plant

carnivore—an animal that eats meat

prey—an animal that is hunted by another animal

scavenger—an animal that eats meat left behind by other hunters

scientist—a person who studies the workings of the world

species—a group of animals who share numerous traits

Read More

Pimentel, Annette Bay. *Do You Really Want to Meet Velociraptor?* Do You Really Want to Meet...? Mankato, Minn.: Amicus Illustrated, 2018.

Raymond, Jayne. *Meet Velociraptor.* The Age of Dinosaurs. New York: Cavendish Square, 2015.

Rissman, Rebecca. *Velociraptor and Other Raptors.* Dinosaur Fact Dig. North Mankato, Minn.: Capstone Press, 2016.

Internet Sites

Use FactHound to find Internet sites related to this book.

Visit www.facthound.com

Just type in 9781515795476 and go.

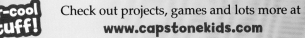
Check out projects, games and lots more at
www.capstonekids.com

Critical Thinking Questions

1. Why do you think velociraptors could not fly?

2. How do scientists know that velociraptors lived in Asia?

3. How do they know that velociraptors ate other dinosaur species?

Index